My
Stories from the Barn Aisle

A prompt journal and guide for writing epic short stories!

Welcome to your new journal!

Here are just a few of the things you'll find in here:

- Pages to help you tell your own horse story
- Journal entry prompts
- Questions about your favorite things
- Doodle pages
- Color pages
- & more!

Let's Go!

If you haven't had a chance to experience real horses yet, no worries! Write about "experiences" from books you've read, or even cooler, create your own fictional adventures! You never know - you might be creating your real future. 🖤

Hi! I'm Sarah, and I'm horse obsessed, (just like you)! My favorite breed is Thoroughbred, and my favorite color is bay roan. My second favorite color is a bright bay like my horse Silas!

I think everyone who has spent time with a horse, even if it was a pony ride at the fair, or riding a stick horse around the yard, has a story to tell. I put a few of mine into a book called Stories from the Barn Aisle, and then I created this journal to help other horse lovers tell their own stories! I hope you enjoy it, and I can't wait to see what you create!

~Sarah

LIFE TALES OF HUMOR AND GRACE FROM A HORSE OBSESSED GIRL

STORIES
from the
BARN
AISLE

SARAH HICKNER

ALL ABOUT ME

My name is
_____

This is a picture of me!

I am _____ years old.

I live in _____

When I'm not riding horses, I like to _____ _____

This is a picture of my favorite horse!

My favorite color horse is
_____

My favorite breed is
_____

My favorite horse discipline is
_____

My favorite treat to give horses is
_____

"I rode a thousand horses before I ever put my foot in a stirrup, all thanks to books."
Sarah Hickner

READING LOG

BOOK: _____

AUTHOR: _____

START DATE: _____   END DATE: _____

BOOK: _____

AUTHOR: _____

START DATE: _____   END DATE: _____

BOOK: _____

AUTHOR: _____

START DATE: _____   END DATE: _____

BOOK: _____

AUTHOR: _____

START DATE: _____   END DATE: _____

BOOK: _____

AUTHOR: _____

START DATE: _____   END DATE: _____

I ♡ horses
I love horses because...

_____
_____
_____
_____
_____
_____
_____
_____
_____
_____
_____
_____
_____
_____
_____
_____
_____
_____
_____
_____
_____
_____
_____

KNOW GROW

List 5 things you know or are good at with horses

List 5 things you'd like to learn or get better at.

 1

 1

 2

 2

 3

 3

 4

 4

5

5

DOODLE PAGE

fun

Would you rather be a world-famous racehorse jockey, jumper rider, or polo player? Choose one, and write a story about winning your biggest competition.

_____
_____
_____
_____
_____
_____
_____
_____
_____
_____
_____
_____
_____
_____
_____
_____
_____
_____
_____

RIDING LESSON REVIEW

COMPLETE THIS AFTER RIDING LESSONS

DATE

WHAT DID I HOPE TO ACCOMPLISH OR LEARN?

WHAT WAS MY ATTITUDE LIKE GOING INTO THE LESSON?

WHAT WAS THE HARDEST PART OF THE LESSON?

WHAT DID I DO BEST?

WHAT WILL I PRACTICE BEFORE MY NEXT LESSON?

DID I REMEMBER TO REWARD MY HORSE FOR ALL OF HIS'HER HARD WORK?

Just Like Mom

My Favorite Horse Day

Draw a picture of your favorite day with a horse – real or imagined! This will be the first step to writing your own story.

My Favorite Horse Day

It's time to start telling your horse story! Let's start with the basics. Imagine one of your favorite horse days...

What was the lesson?

Who was with you?

What time of day and year did it happen?

Where did it take place?

Why was it important?

Describe
"My Favorite Horse Day"
with your five senses.

This will help the story feel real to the reader.

looks	feels	smells	sounds	tastes

"My Favorite Horse Day"
Parts of the story
Take some time to identify these three parts of your story.

Conflict – this is the struggle you are working to overcome. It could be convincing your parents to let you ride, having a hard time learning to post the trot, or overcoming a fear. The conflict is the core of the story.

Climax - this is the point of greatest tension where your conflict gets the most difficult - your parents are deciding if you can ride, you've been bounced around at the trot so much you almost fall off and you want to give up, the thing you fear the most starts to happen.

Resolution - the end of the story where the conflict is resolved - your parents schedule your riding lesson, you victoriously post an entire lap around the riding ring, you faced your fear and lived to tell the story!

"My Favorite Horse Day"

Are you ready? I believe you are! Using all the things you've prepared, it's time to piece it together and write your story.

_____

_____

_____

_____

_____

_____

_____

_____

_____

_____

_____

_____

_____

_____

_____

_____

_____

DOODLE PAGE

smile

Make a playlist of songs for the barn!

- _____
- _____
- _____
- _____
- _____
- _____
- _____
- _____
- _____
- _____

Poetry Corner

Cinquain

A Cinquain is a five-lined poem. It is easy to write, and fun to read!

_____
Line 1: a noun (what the poem is about)

_____ _____
Line 2: 2 adjectives that describe Line 1

_____ _____ _____
Line 3: 3 -ing action verbs related to Line 1

_____ _____ _____ _____
Line 4: 4 words to make a phrase or sentence that relates to Line 1

_____
Line 5: 1 synonym for Line 1

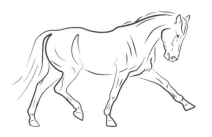

example: Horse
Handsome bay
Nuzzling, trotting, jumping
Makes my heart happy
Silas

"Jobs of the Horse World" Crossword Puzzle

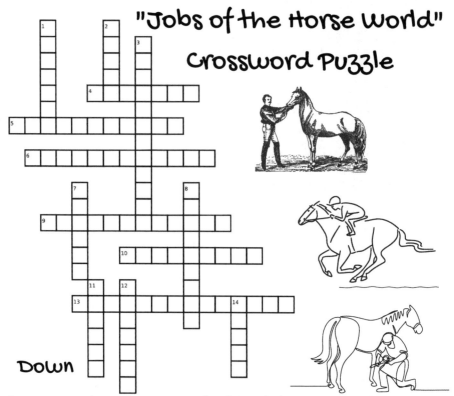

Down

1. Someone who takes care of a horse's hooves.
2. The person at a horse show who chooses the winners.
3. An artist who takes pictures of horses.
7. Someone who communicates with the written word.
8. A person who walks horses at the racetrack.
11. A racehorse rider.
12. A teacher for horses, riders, or both.
14. The person who takes care of the horse's well-being and appearance for shows or the racetrack.

Across

4. A person who takes care of a horse's teeth.
5. A person who manages the workings of a barn.
6. A doctor for horses and other animals.
9. A person who adjusts the horse's spine to keep it in alignment
10. A person who does therapies for horses such as massage.
13. Someone who designs jumping courses for horse shows.

"Show Don't Tell"

In the writing world there is a saying, "show don't tell." It refers to using descriptive words to create an image of the story in the reader's mind instead of simply telling it. I'll use this page to give examples, and on the next page you can practice!

Tell: The horse was nervous.
show:

The mare's body trembled as a white rim appeared around her eyes.

Tell: Silas was hungry.
show:

Silas pawed at his feed bucket, banging the plastic, as he anticipated dinner.

Tell: Posting the trot was hard.
show:

My trainer said, "stand and then sit!" But I was bouncing all over the saddle.

Tell: It was early morning.
show:

When I arrived at the barn the sun was barely awake and I wished I had a jacket.

Tell: I was so annoyed.
show:

I grit my teeth together, slowly breathing to keep from yelling.

"Show Don't Tell"

Your turn!

Tell: The horse was excited!

show:

Tell: Clyde was thirsty.

show:

Tell: The bridle was confusing.

show:

Tell: It was late afternoon.

show:

Tell: I was hungry.

show:

MY FAVORITES

List some of your favorite things from the barn!

BARN SMELLS

- [ ] horse peppermint breath
- [ ] _____
- [ ] _____
- [ ] _____
- [ ] _____
- [ ] _____

BARN SOUNDS

- [ ] horses eating
- [ ] _____
- [ ] _____
- [ ] _____
- [ ] _____
- [ ] _____

BARN FEELS

- [ ] horse whiskers when they sniff my hand
- [ ] _____
- [ ] _____
- [ ] _____
- [ ] _____
- [ ] _____

DOODLE PAGE

persist

Write about a time you laughed so hard you couldn't breathe!

_____

_____

_____

_____

_____

_____

_____

_____

_____

_____

_____

_____

_____

_____

_____

_____

_____

_____

_____

_____

_____

_____

RIDING LESSON REVIEW

DATE

WHAT DID I HOPE TO ACCOMPLISH OR LEARN?

WHAT WAS MY ATTITUDE LIKE GOING INTO THE LESSON?

WHAT WAS THE HARDEST PART OF THE LESSON?

WHAT DID I DO BEST?

WHAT WILL I PRACTICE BEFORE MY NEXT LESSON?

DID I REMEMBER TO REWARD MY HORSE FOR ALL OF HIS/HER HARD WORK?

Life isn't all sunshine and rainbows. Write about the hardest part of loving horses.

_____
_____
_____
_____
_____
_____
_____
_____
_____
_____
_____
_____
_____
_____
_____
_____
_____
_____
_____
_____
_____
_____
_____

My Horse's Favorite Treats

List your horse's favorite treats. If you don't ride a horse yet, list the treats you'd most like to give a horse!

1. ←————————————————————→

2. ←————————————————————→

3. ←————————————————————→

4. ←————————————————————→

5. ←————————————————————→

6. ←————————————————————→

7. ←————————————————————→

"Reading is essential for those who seek to rise above the ordinary." - Jim Rohn

READING LOG

BOOK: _____

AUTHOR: _____

START DATE: _____ END DATE: _____

BOOK: _____

AUTHOR: _____

START DATE: _____ END DATE: _____

BOOK: _____

AUTHOR: _____

START DATE: _____ END DATE: _____

BOOK: _____

AUTHOR: _____

START DATE: _____ END DATE: _____

BOOK: _____

AUTHOR: _____

START DATE: _____ END DATE: _____

A Lesson I Learned

Draw a picture from a day you learned an important horse lesson! It could be something like learning not to give up, learning to forgive your horse, or even learning the hard way to keep your hand flat when you give a treat!

A Lesson I Learned

It's time to start telling another horse story! Let's start with the basics. Imagine a lesson you've learned the hard way with a horse...

What was the lesson?

Who was with you?

What time of day and year did it happen?

Where did it take place?

Why was it important?

Describe
"A Lesson I Learned"
with your five senses.

This will help the story feel real to the reader.

looks	feels	smells	sounds	tastes

"A Lesson I Learned"
PARTS OF THE STORY
Take some time to identify these three parts of your story.

Conflict – this is the struggle you are working to overcome. It could be convincing your parents to let you ride, having a hard time learning to post the trot, or overcoming a fear. The conflict is the core of the story.

Climax – this is the point of greatest tension where your conflict gets the most difficult – your parents are deciding if you can ride, you've been bounced around at the trot so much you almost fall off and you want to give up, the thing you fear the most starts to happen'

Resolution – the end of the story where the conflict is resolved – your parents schedule your riding lesson, you victoriously post an entire lap around the riding ring, you faced your fear and lived to tell the story!

"A Lesson I Learned"

Are you ready? I believe you are! Using all the things you've prepared, it's time to write your story.

_____

_____

_____

_____

_____

_____

_____

_____

_____

_____

_____

_____

_____

_____

_____

Color to look like your favorite horse!

DOODLE PAGE

Learn

Write a letter to either your favorite horse or your dream horse.

_____

_____

_____

_____

_____

_____

_____

_____

_____

_____

_____

_____

_____

_____

_____

_____

_____

_____

_____

_____

_____

_____

_____

Tape or draw a picture of one of your best barn days!

Best DAY ever!

DOODLE PAGE

dream

If you could own any horse in the world who would you own and why?

_____
_____
_____
_____
_____
_____
_____
_____
_____
_____
_____
_____
_____
_____
_____
_____
_____
_____
_____
_____
_____
_____
_____

Scrambled

Unscramble the words, then draw a line to match the word with its discipline.

VNIIRD6 _____

nriigne _____

oolp _____

egsrsade _____

gujnipm _____

nrigop _____

lrareb granic _____

Poetry Corner

Haiku

A haiku is an unrhymed three-line poem. The traditional pattern in English is to write the first and last lines with five syllables each, and the middle line with seven syllables.

Line 1: 5 syllables
Line 2: 7 syllables
Line 3: 5 syllables

example:
Silas munches hay.
He blinks the dust from his eyes.
It's a lazy day.

Try writing a couple Haikus of your own!

DOODLE PAGE

believe

Feel Important

"Pretend that everyone has a sign around their neck that says make me feel important"

~Mary Kay Ash

THINGS PEOPLE HAVE SAID THAT MADE YOU FEEL IMPORTANT

1. ....

2. ....

3. ....

THINGS YOU CAN SAY TO OTHERS TO MAKE THEM FEEL IMPORANT

1. ....

2. ....

3. ....

WHO WOULD YOU LOVE TO ENCOURAGE?

DOODLE PAGE

Work Hard

"Hey Little Buddy"

RIDING LESSON REVIEW

COMPLETE THIS AFTER RIDING LESSONS

DATE

WHAT DID I HOPE TO ACCOMPLISH OR LEARN?

WHAT WAS MY ATTITUDE LIKE GOING INTO THE LESSON?

WHAT WAS THE HARDEST PART OF THE LESSON?

WHAT DID I DO BEST?

WHAT WILL I PRACTICE BEFORE MY NEXT LESSON?

DID I REMEMBER TO REWARD MY HORSE FOR ALL OF HIS'HER HARD WORK?

My Horse Goals

THINGS I WANT TO LEARN

plan it out

THINGS I WANT TO ACHIEVE

THINGS I WANT TO DO

OTHER GOALS

Writing with Strong Verbs

A verb is the action word in a sentence: run, walk, think, talk, sit, stand, go. Most people write using simple verbs, and then add something called an adverb to describe it: run fast, walk slow, talk loud.

One technique for improving creative writing is using strong verbs. A strong verb conveys the picture or feeling without needing descriptive words: sprint, trudge, yell.

Examples:

weak: Gideon ran really fast.
strong: Gideon sprinted.

weak: Waylon stepped quickly into the mud puddle.
strong: Waylon plunged into the mud puddle.

Practice

Rewrite these sentences and make them better using strong verbs.

The horse walked excitedly down the path.

_____

The horse jumped away from the barking dog and ran away.

_____

Writing with Strong Verbs

more practice!

Flip back through the journal and find sentences with weak verbs. Copy them into the box, and then rewrite using strong verbs.

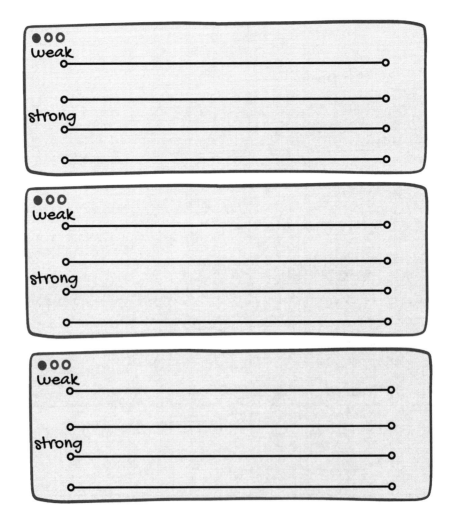

● ○ ○
weak

strong

● ○ ○
weak

strong

● ○ ○
weak

strong

Silly Horse Stories

Without looking at the next page, fill in the blanks for the following words. Once you're done, insert the words into the coordinating number space on the next page and read the story.

(1) girl name _____

(2) adjective _____

(3) exclamation _____

(4) famous guy _____

(5) adjective _____

(6) mood _____

(7) noun _____

(8) food _____

(9) verb ending in -ing _____

(10) adjective _____

Silly Horse Stories

_____ was the most

1

_____ horse in the barn.

2

Whenever people went by her stall they

said _____!

3

One day, _____ was in

4

town and came to see this _____

5

horse. He was so _____ that

6

he immediately offered _____

7

to take that horse home.

When they arrived, he gave the horse

_____. The horse thanked him

8

by _____ him on the face.

9

They lived _____ily ever after.

10

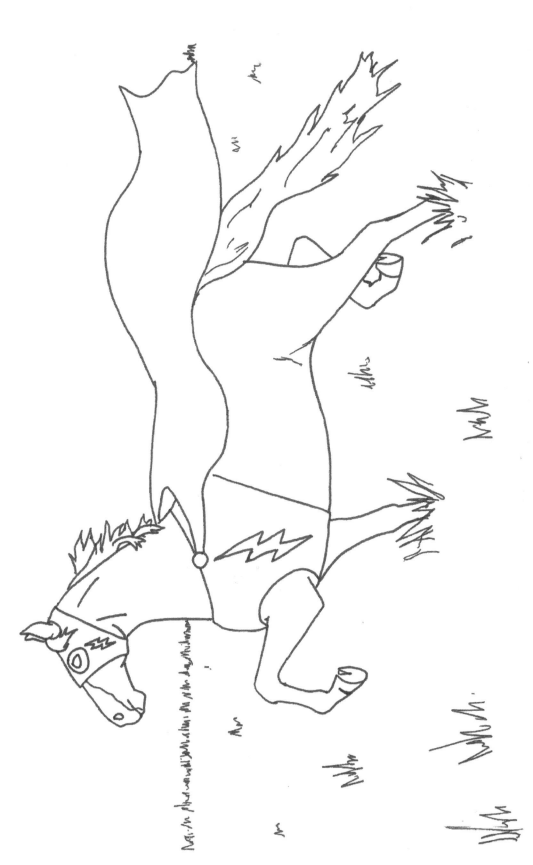

RIDING LESSON REVIEW

COMPLETE THIS AFTER RIDING LESSONS

DATE

WHAT DID I HOPE TO ACCOMPLISH OR LEARN?

WHAT WAS MY ATTITUDE LIKE GOING INTO THE LESSON?

WHAT WAS THE HARDEST PART OF THE LESSON?

WHAT DID I DO BEST?

WHAT WILL I PRACTICE BEFORE MY NEXT LESSON?

DID I REMEMBER TO REWARD MY HORSE FOR ALL OF HIS'HER HARD WORK?

Horse Breeds Word Search

```
S A D D L E B R E D T Y T C D Z T Y F P
K K L I P I Z Z A N E R I U F R E E C E
P M T L S Z P P E R C H E R O N D J A F
J O F F Q G K P A D D I T R P L T V A R
A C J E A P U R M C A L O I D M C W Z L
R P X X G X T L W B X Z L Z T B X A J C
F X P Q U A R T E R H O R S E W R N C M
M D A A P S O T B P M F Z C J A H D P U
U Q P R L K K N H C A L K Q Z R P A P S
Y K Q A A O R F S O J J V J F M S L N T
J M K F I B O V C N R Y V V R B G U A A
Q O N R M N I S L N D O W S F L Q S B N
F R N I Q X T A A E T I U Y X O V I C G
I G D E R G T H N M I Q M G C O J A H R
O A F S D S N F O A B N C L H D K N G J
S N A I Y B X A K R G E E X X B Y L E V
B D C A T Z Q K C A S T E R U N R P Q M
L D N N D R J E W S Z E J W E E Q E Y T
J B S B P A S O F I N O M J K F K O D A
C L Y D E S D A L E Q W R Z G Q Y M T S
```

Thoroughbred	Quarter Horse	Paint Horse	Andalusian
Saddlebred	Clydesdale	Lipizzaner	Appaloosa
Percheron	Paso Fino	Friesian	Mustang
Warmblood	Arabian	Connemara	Morgan

Story Ideas

Write ideas for other horse stories you'd love to write!

IMAGINE YOU ARE A HORSE
SITTING IN A STALL OR FIELD
ALL DAY. WHAT WOULD YOU
THINK ABOUT?

_____
_____
_____
_____
_____
_____
_____
_____
_____
_____
_____
_____
_____
_____
_____
_____
_____
_____
_____
_____
_____
_____
_____
_____

"The more that you read, the more things you will know. The more that you learn, the more places you'll go." - Dr. Seuss

READING LOG

BOOK: _____

AUTHOR: _____

START DATE: _____ END DATE: _____

BOOK: _____

AUTHOR: _____

START DATE: _____ END DATE: _____

BOOK: _____

AUTHOR: _____

START DATE: _____ END DATE: _____

BOOK: _____

AUTHOR: _____

START DATE: _____ END DATE: _____

BOOK: _____

AUTHOR: _____

START DATE: _____ END DATE: _____

Choose a story from your story ideas page
(it's 3 pages back).

title: _____

Draw a picture from the story to help your brain
start imagining all the details.

Title: _____

It's time to start telling your horse story! Let's start with the basics.

What was the lesson?

Who was with you?

What time of day and year did it happen?

Where did it take place?

Why was it important?

Describe
your story
with your five senses.

This will help the story feel real to the reader.

looks	feels	smells	sounds	tastes

Title:_____

PARTS OF THE STORY

Take some time to identify these three parts of your story.

Conflict - this is the struggle you are working to overcome. It could be convincing your parents to let you ride, having a hard time learning to post the trot, or overcoming a fear. The conflict is the core of the story.

Climax - this is the point of greatest tension where your conflict gets the most difficult - your parents are deciding if you can ride, you've been bounced around at the trot so much you almost fall off and you want to give up, the thing you fear the most starts to happen.

Resolution - the end of the story where the conflict is resolved - your parents schedule your riding lesson, you victoriously post an entire lap around the riding ring, you faced your fear and lived to tell the story

Title: _____

Are you ready? I believe you are! Using all the things you've prepared, it's time to write your story.

_____

_____

_____

_____

_____

_____

_____

_____

_____

_____

_____

_____

_____

_____

_____

_____

DOODLE PAGE

Help Others

RIDING LESSON REVIEW

COMPLETE THIS AFTER RIDING LESSONS

DATE

WHAT DID I HOPE TO
ACCOMPLISH OR LEARN?

WHAT WAS MY ATTITUDE LIKE
GOING INTO THE LESSON?

WHAT WAS THE HARDEST PART
OF THE LESSON?

WHAT DID I DO BEST?

WHAT WILL I PRACTICE BEFORE
MY NEXT LESSON?

DID I REMEMBER TO REWARD MY
HORSE FOR ALL OF HIS'HER
HARD WORK?

5 THINGS AT THE BARN THAT MAKE ME SMILE

▷

▷

▷

▷

▷

THANK YOU

Write a thank-you note to someone who has encouraged or inspired you in your horse journey. Then rewrite it on a notecard or tear it out of the journal and send it to him or her!

What's your favorite horse book and why?

_____

_____

_____

_____

_____

_____

_____

_____

_____

_____

_____

_____

_____

_____

_____

_____

_____

_____

_____

_____

_____

_____

_____

Poetry Corner
Acrostic

Acrostic poems are simple and fun! You choose something you want to write about (I'll choose "Silas"), then write the word vertically.
Using the letters from your word as a starting place, write a word or sentence to describe your subject.

example: "Silas"

Stoic unless he's spooking at a log

Irritable when I groom him

Lazy when we're in the ring

Acrobatic when he doesn't get out enough

Special to me

I did the sentence version because it made me laugh! But here is a version with just a word:

"Silas"
Stoic
Irritable
Lazy
Acrobatic
Special

Poetry Corner
Acrostic

Your turn!

Write your own acrostic poem (or five).

Add a photo or illustration if you want.

Create your perfect horse day, and write all about it.

A ride on the beach? A clinic with your hero? A blue ribbon at the show? Moonlit trail ride? You may need extra pages!

_____

_____

_____

_____

_____

_____

_____

_____

_____

_____

_____

_____

_____

_____

_____

_____

_____

_____

_____

_____

_____

_____

Grow

write your own horse comic strip

TITLE _____

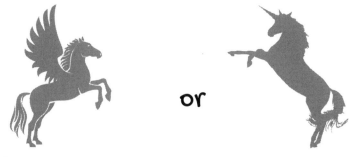

or

If you could choose, would you rather ride
Pegasus or a unicorn?
Write about it! What adventures would you go on?

_____
_____
_____
_____
_____
_____
_____
_____
_____
_____
_____
_____
_____
_____
_____
_____
_____
_____
_____

List your Favorite Horse Names

females

males

_____

_____

_____

_____

_____

_____

_____

_____

_____

_____

_____

_____

_____

_____

_____

_____

_____

_____

_____

_____

_____

_____

Have you ever dreamed of writing your own horse book?

Create a cover for your book!

Becoming a Great Writer

Something they don't always tell you in school (or maybe they tell you, but I didn't hear), is the best books have been written and rewritten, fixed, read, and fixed some more.

WE CALL THIS PROCESS "REVISION."

It's quite a process!

When I started writing for other people, I wanted the first version to be perfect. In fact, I was convinced it was already a masterpiece! Newsflash to my past self: It was not even close to a masterpiece. I might even call it bad.

Now, I love revising! It's so fun to see your work evolve.

Look back into some of the journal entries or stories you've written, and use the next page and a half to rewrite all or part of one. You may cut out extra words, use stronger verbs, or see that you were "telling" the story but now you can "show" it with your words.

_____

_____

_____

_____

_____

_____

_____

DOODLE PAGE

Practice

Parts of the Horse

See if you can label the parts of the horse!
The answer key is in the back of the book.

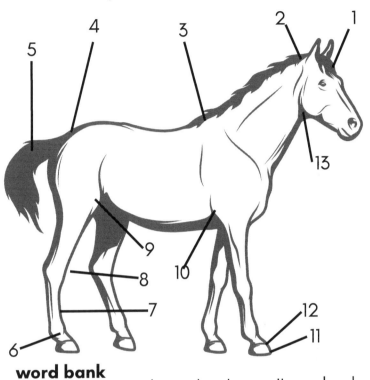

word bank

dock	coronet	throat latch	poll	hock
elbow	cannon	withers	hoof	
tail	forehead	fetlock	stifle	

1. _____
2. _____
3. _____
4. _____
5. _____
6. _____
7. _____

8. _____
9. _____
10. _____
11. _____
12. _____
13. _____

RIDING LESSON REVIEW

DATE

WHAT DID I HOPE TO ACCOMPLISH OR LEARN?

WHAT WAS MY ATTITUDE LIKE GOING INTO THE LESSON?

WHAT WAS THE HARDEST PART OF THE LESSON?

WHAT DID I DO BEST?

WHAT WILL I PRACTICE BEFORE MY NEXT LESSON?

DID I REMEMBER TO REWARD MY HORSE FOR ALL OF HIS'HER HARD WORK?

Hey friend,

You've made it to the end! Congratulations!!! I'm guessing if you've gotten this far in the journal you are definitely horse obsessed.

I can so relate! I remember devouring horse books and thinking if I could just ride a horse, all my dreams would come true. Then I finally got to start riding and I thought, if I could have a horse of my own I'd never want anything else!

Some trust in chariots and some in horses, but we trust in the name of the Lord our God.
PSALM 20:7
LiveRideLearn.com

I want to share something from my heart. There's this verse in the Bible that says, "Some trust in chariots and others in horses, but we trust in the name of the Lord our God." (from Psalm 20:7)

The first time I read that I thought, why shouldn't I trust in horses?! They're the best!

But every time I achieved a horse dream, it was never enough. I got to take riding lessons, and I wanted more. I got my own horse, and I wanted more! I got to show and take a horse to college. Basically, whatever I wanted (with a lot of determination) I tried, and it was never enough.

Here's the problem—horses, while amazing gifts from God, are still only animals. Most of the time they're incredible, but sometimes they buck you off, or choose their friends or food over you.

No matter how much you get, you'll want more. One day you'll probably go out to the barn and your favorite horse will be hurt, and sometimes they pass away and leave us empty.

A long time ago my most favorite horse in the world broke his leg, and I thought my life would end if he didn't make it. In the days when I was waiting to see if Gideon would live or not, God showed me that I didn't need a horse to survive. I needed to trust in my creator.

So I just want to encourage you as you go forward with your horses. I hope and pray that you get everything you can imagine in your horse dreams, but just remember that even if you make it to the Olympics on the best horse in the world, it will never fill your heart like the love of Jesus does.

These animals are gifts from God, so if you're choosing whom to trust, I recommend trusting the one who created them.

Happy Trails,
Sarah

MY FAVORITES

What was your favorite activity from the journal?

Which 3 pages are you most proud of?

What surprised you from the journal?

Did you or will you share some of your work with a teacher, friend, or parent?

What are your plans to keep growing as a rider or writer?

Draw or write something that makes you smile :)

Enjoy some blank pages - no rules or expectations!
Just have fun!

Did you write a story, journal entry, or poem that you're super proud of? I'd love to see it! Email it to me (Sarah) at StoriesFromTheBarnAisle@gmail.com

If you loved this journal, do me the biggest favor and leave a review on Amazon!

Have you read
Stories from the Barn Aisle?

In Sarah's debut book, she shares five
hilarious true stories from her adventures
with horses. It will leave you craving
more horsehair in your life!
Available in paperback, ebook, and
audio!

FREE Short Story!

Sarah and her fiancé are back home for a couple of weeks for a very special occasion — their wedding. But will an accident with the beautiful steed Joey is supposed to ride on their wedding day ruin all her little girl dreams?

For your free short story and updates on Sarah's book releases, sign up for her monthly newsletter at www.LiveRideLearn.com/freeshortstory

Answer Key

Horse Breeds Word Search

```
S A D D L E B R E D T Y T C D Z T Y F P
K K L I P I Z Z A N E R I U F R E E C E
P M T L S Z P P E R C H E R O N D J A F
J O F F Q G K P A D D I T R P L T V A R
A C J E A P U R M C A L O I D M C W Z L
R P X X G X T L W B X Z L Z T B X A J C
F X P Q U A R T E R H O R S E W R N C M
M D A A P S O T B P M F Z C J A H D P U
U Q P R L K K N H C A L K Q Z R P A P S
Y K Q A A O R F S O J J V J F M S L N T
J M K F I B Q V C N R Y V V R B G U A A
Q O N R M N S L N D O W S F L Q S B N C
F R N I Q X T A A E T I U Y X O V I C G
I G D E R G T H W M I Q M G C O J A H R
O A F S D S N F Q A B N C L H D K N G J
S W A I Y B X A K R G E E X X B Y L E V
B D C A T Z Q K C A S T E R U N R P Q M
L D N N D R J E W S Z E J W E E Q E Y T
J B S B P A S O F I N O M J K F K O D A
C L Y D E S D A L E Q W R Z G Q Y M T S
```

Parts of the Horse

1. forehead
2. poll
3. withers
4. dock
5. tail
6. fetlock
7. cannon
8. hock
9. stifle
10. elbow
11. hoof
12. coronet
13. throat latch

Scrambled

Unscramble the words, then match the word with its discipline

VNIIRDG   driving

nriigne   reining

oolp   polo

egsrsade   dressage

gujnipm   jumping

nrigop   roping

lrareb granic   barrel racing

Jobs of the Horse World

```
      F           U     P
      A           U     H
      R           D     O
      R       D E N T I S T
      I           G     O
B A R N M A N A G E R
      V E T E R I N A R I A N
      |           P
      W       H   H
      R       E   O
  C H I R O P R A C T O R
      T       A   W
      E     T H E R A P I S T
      R     |     L
      |     |     K
  C O U R S E D E S I G N E R
      C     A     R
      K     I     O
      E     N     O
      Y     E     M
            R
```

Made in the USA
Middletown, DE
18 May 2022